Oh! No!

Not the Anchovy!

THE NUMBER OF PLAYERS:

2-4

THE OBJECT OF THE GAME: To land on the big pizza.

THE PLAYING PIECES: One different playing piece for each player; one pair of dice.

THE PLAY: Players take turns throwing the dice, adding the two numbers, and moving forward that number of spaces. If a player throws a double, he or she gets another turn. If a player lands on an occupied space, he or she sends that piece to the nearest corner.

THE WINNER: The player who lands first on the big pizza wins. The exact number is not needed for a player to win, however. For example, if a player needs to throw a 5, and he or she throws a 7, that player may move forward to win.

MATH CONCEPTS: Addition with sums from 2 to 12. Shape recognition: square, circle, triangle, rectangle, octagon.

HOW DO OCTOPI EAT PIZZA PIE?

PIZZA MATH

TIME LIFE *for* Children™

ALEXANDRIA, VIRGINIA

ALL ABOUT
I LOVE MATH!

Come join the pickle party on page 20!

Dear Parent,

The *I Love Math* series shows children that math is all around them in everything they do. It can be found at the grocery store, at a soccer game, in the kitchen, at the zoo, even in their own bodies. As you collect this series, each book will fill in another piece of your child's world, showing how math is a natural part of everyday activities.

What is Math?

Math is much more than manipulating numbers; the goal of math education today is to help children become problem solvers. This means teaching kids to observe the world around them by looking for patterns and relationships, estimating, measuring, comparing, and using reasoning skills. From an early age, children do this naturally. They divide up cookies to share with friends, recognize shapes in pizza, measure how tall they have grown, or match colors and patterns as they dress themselves. Young children love math. But when math only takes the form of abstract formulas on worksheets, children begin to dislike it. The *I Love Math* series is designed to keep math natural and appealing.

How Do Children Learn Math?

Research has shown that children learn best by doing. Therefore, *I Love Math* is a hands-on, interactive learning experience. The math concepts are woven into stories in which entertaining characters invite your child to help them solve math challenges. Activities reinforce the concepts, and parent notes offer ways you and your child can have more fun with this program.

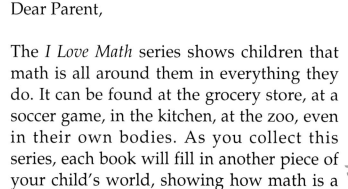

Help solve a pizza mystery on page 30.

We have worked closely with math educators to include in these books a full range of math skills. As the series progresses, repetition of these skills in different formats will help your child master the basics of mathematical thinking.

How Can You Help Your Child?
Some of the math challenges will be easy for your child; some will be harder. Encourage your child to work at his or her own pace. Praise your child's efforts whether or not the answer is correct, emphasizing that the right approach is often more important than the right answer.

And as you read this book with your child, remember the adage:

Tell me and I forget.
Show me and I remember.
Involve me and I understand.
Encourage me and I want to keep learning.

If you do encourage and praise your child's efforts, you both can say:

I LOVE MATH!

The Editors
Time-Life for Children

Turn to page 42 to find out how we butterflies count french fries.

Table of Contents

How do octopi eat pizza pie?

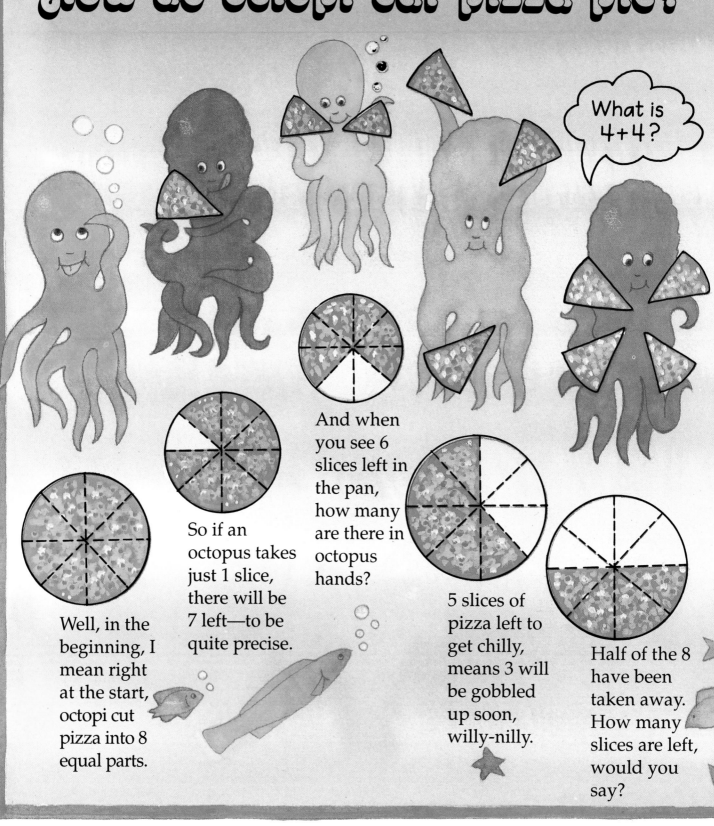

What is 4 + 4 ?

Well, in the beginning, I mean right at the start, octopi cut pizza into 8 equal parts.

So if an octopus takes just 1 slice, there will be 7 left—to be quite precise.

And when you see 6 slices left in the pan, how many are there in octopus hands?

5 slices of pizza left to get chilly, means 3 will be gobbled up soon, willy-nilly.

Half of the 8 have been taken away. How many slices are left, would you say?

MATH FOCUS: ADDITION AND SUBTRACTION. By describing what happens in this poem, children practice addition and subtraction. Talk about each scene. Ask your child to tell how many pizza slices were in the pan to begin with, how many the octopus took, and how many are left. Then look at the story again, moving from right to left. Have your child tell how many slices are in the pan, how many the octopus is holding, and how many there are in all.

6

What is the name for the number that means none?

7 are gone, with 1 slice remaining. Didn't that take a lot of explaining?

3 in the pan, not more and not less. How many are missing? Take a good guess.

2 slices of pizza. My, what a fix! A pizza pie lover must have eaten up 6.

This poem is finished. What? You say "No." The pan is now empty? How can that be so? There's nothing. There's zero. Where did those 8 go?

MORE FUN. Help your child do this activity. On a piece of paper, trace around a plate. Cut out the circle. Color it like a pizza. Fold it in half, in half again, and in half again. Cut out the 8 "slices" and act out the poem.

Elephant Juice

Hector and Ellen were twin brother and sister.
They lived with their parents in Elephantchister.
And though they were two of the nicest kids ever,
They did have a problem—each had to be better.

If one shelled some peanuts, the other shelled more,
Till they spilled out of the bowl and onto the floor.
If one picked four roses to put in the den,
The other came back from the garden with ten.
They'd look and they'd count until one twin said, "Yes!
See! I have six more! You have six less!"

MATH FOCUS: CAPACITY. By seeing how much liquid two bottles hold, children learn to compare capacities of containers, a fundamental measurement skill. Talk about how much the containers seen in this story might hold in relation to each other. Have your child guess which twin's container holds more juice.

8

One day the whole family piled into its car,
And drove to the store, which was not very far.
One twin took a cart from the group near the door.
The other took three carts, just to have more!

Hector and Ellen both loved to go shopping.
They bought apple tree bark and bamboo cake topping,
Seven sugar cane patties, nine dandelion flakes,
Straw salad, grass soup, and eight coconut shakes.

MORE FUN. Have your child find pairs of containers that look different but that hold the same amount—for example, a short, fat 16-ounce bottle and a tall, thin 16-ounce bottle.

9

They were waiting in line behind Mr. Moose,
When Ellen said, "Mom, may we pick out some juice?"
Said Mom, "You may each get the kind you like best."
That pleased the twins, as you've probably guessed!
So while Mom and Dad asked the Mooses their news,
Hector and Ellen rushed right off to choose.

They saw bottles and cartons, aluminum cans,
With pictures and labels from faraway lands.
Some containers were big, some containers were small,
Some containers were short, some containers were tall,
Some containers were thin, some containers were wide,
All those containers on shelves, side by side.

Hmmm.... Which one has the most sugar in it?

1 Pound

2 Pounds

3 Pounds

There was fresh Lemon Peel and Maple Leaf Fizzle,
Acorn Delight, and some green Grassy Swizzle.
"Oh, golly! Gee whiz! Oh, my goodness!" said Hector,
"Hmmm, what should I get? I'll take Peanut Nectar!"
He reached for a bottle; it was tall, trim, and thin,
Then he looked down the aisle till he spotted his twin.
She had a juice called Orange Tree Pop.
It came in a bottle short, fat, and squat.

"She doesn't have much," Hector thought with delight.
"My bottle holds more, and I'm sure that I'm right!"
Then Ellen examined both of their choices.
"His holds less!" she said in the softest of voices.

11

That evening at dinner the twins sat in their places,
And looked at their juices—big smiles on their faces.
Father was puzzled; he finally spoke,
"Why are you smiling? Do tell us the joke!"

"My bottle holds more—it's so tall!" Hector said.
His twin said, "You're wrong!" and then shook her head.
"It's as plain as the nose on your face," Ellen said, "that
My bottle holds more because it's so fat!"
They argued and argued till Mother stepped in.
"Get your glass," she said to each angry twin.

"Hector, open your nectar. Ellen, open your pop.
And pour the juice out, but don't spill a drop!"
They poured and they poured, not a bit did remain.
The amount in each glass was exactly the same!

"Oh, wow!" said the sister. "Gee whiz!" said the brother.
"Let's check again," they said to each other.
"The bottles look different. Let's make it a game,
To find out for sure if they both hold the same."

"Pour your juice into my bottle," said Ellen with glee.
"I'll pour mine into yours, and then we will see."
They each used a funnel. No juice was spilled.
Both of those bottles were completely filled.
"Oh, yes!" said Ellen. "It's true!" said her brother.
And they smiled and smiled, their arms round one another.

14

TRY THIS!

Get two empty containers.

When you fill both, will they hold the same amount ?

Maybe one will hold more, and the other will hold less. Take a guess!

FILL ONE!

Use cereal.

Pour the cereal into the other container.

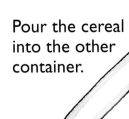

WHAT HAPPENED?

Now compare capacities of other empty containers. How much does each hold? Use water if you want to.

MATH FOCUS: CAPACITY. As you do this activity, use the terms **holds more, holds less,** and **holds the same amount.**

15

MORE FUN. Help your child ask family members to guess which of each pair of containers holds more and which holds less, or if they both hold the same amount.

Take a Guess!

Guess about how many are in the bowl!

MATH FOCUS: ESTIMATION, CAPACITY. By estimating how many fish crackers there are in a bowl, children develop important thinking strategies in their effort toward making a reasonably accurate guess.

Discuss the fact that this is a photograph of a real three-dimensional fish bowl and that there are more fish in it than we can see.

1,000,000

280,000

Which of these numbers comes closest to the number of 🐟 in the bowl?

25

10

3,000,000

MORE FUN. Have your child guess about how many raisins there are in a small box or about how many pieces of candy there are in a small bag. Then have him or her check by counting.

ANSWER. There are 992 fish crackers in the bowl. Any guess within a few hundred is reasonable. Of the numbers shown, 1,000 comes closest to the actual number in the bowl.

How do poodles use their noodles?

Mrs. Poodle hoped to go,

To Westminister's Kennel Show.

There she'd take her poodle litter,

To win a prize all trimmed with glitter.

From the rule book she had found,

Each pup must weigh at least one pound.

She wondered how to weigh her poodles.

Then she spied a crate of noodles.

"Each box weighs one pound, I know.

I'll check their weight before the show."

With one box, the scale was balanced.

Just one pound weighed wiggly Clarence.

Spot weighed three pounds; Tip weighed one.

The puppies sure were having fun!

Alice sat with Tip and Spot.

They weighed six pounds—now that's a lot.

I think I weigh 2 pounds. What do you think?

MATH FOCUS: WEIGHT. Children are introduced to the process of measuring by comparing weights of puppies to one-pound boxes instead of to standard weights. Discuss what "the scale was balanced" means—that whatever is on the left side of the scale weighs the same as whatever is on the right. Take turns making up and answering other questions by using the data on the graph.

Max weighed two. As you can see,

Adding Fifi balanced three.

Mom was sure her pups could win.

Now she knew they weren't too thin.

She was right—they were judged the best.

They weighed enough. They passed the test.

How smart it was of Mrs. Poodle,

To weigh her pups and use her noodle!

MORE FUN. Get a five-pound bag of sugar or flour. Have your child find objects around the house that he or she thinks weigh as much. Compare their weights using a bathroom scale.

Pickle Party

Dilly was so excited! It was time to open her birthday present from Uncle Picklepuss. Dilly's cousin helped her untie the big red satin bow on the huge box. They could hardly wait to see what was inside.

MATH FOCUS: PATTERNS AND RELATIONSHIPS. By analyzing what goes into a function machine and what comes out of it, children learn to recognize patterns and relationships, a fundamental principle underlying mathematical operations. Tell your child that finding each order is like finding the reason why the objects that go in and come out "go together."

"Oh, it's an FM," said Dilly in delight.

"Is it a radio?" asked her cousin.

"Don't be silly, Piccalilli. It's a Function Machine. It's called FM for short. You can tell it to do almost anything. Just put an order into this slot. You'll see."

MORE FUN. Encourage your child to make up his or her own orders for the function machine, telling what he or she would put into the machine and then telling what would come out.

Dilly puts an order into the left side of the FM. Piccalilli waits on the right side.

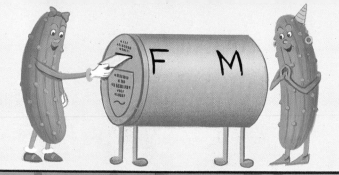

Dilly puts a pizza into the FM.

What is Piccalilli taking out of the FM?

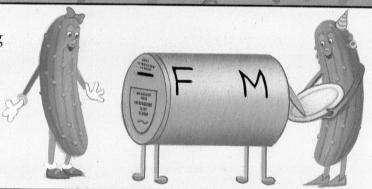

What is Dilly putting into the FM this time?

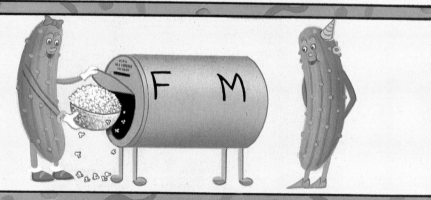

What is Piccalilli taking out of the FM this time?

What order did Dilly give to the machine?

Dilly puts an order into the left side of the FM. Piccalilli waits on the right side.

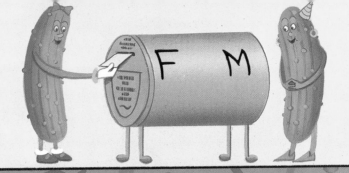

Dilly puts a banana into the FM.

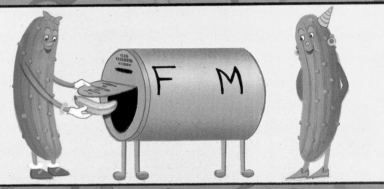

What happened?

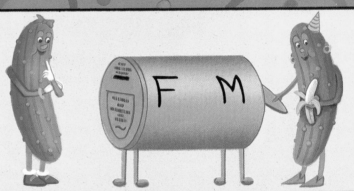

Tell what Dilly is doing.

Tell what happened.

What order did Dilly give to the machine?

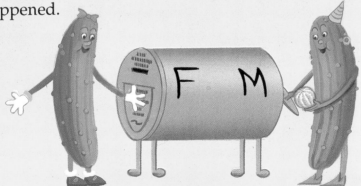

23

 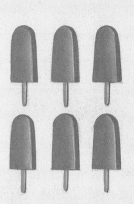

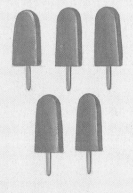 

 *What order did the machine follow?*

24

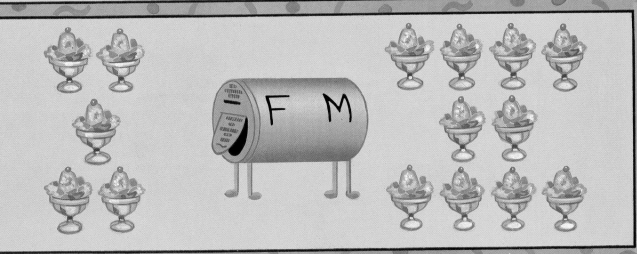

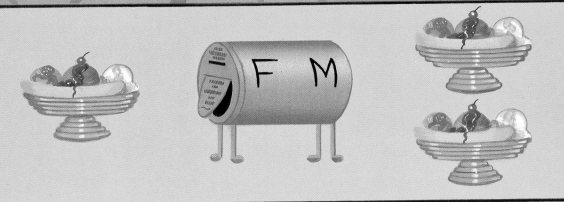

What order did the machine follow?

25

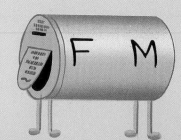

 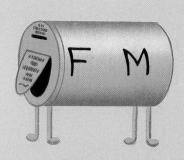 

What order did the machine follow?

If 3 is put in, what number will come out?

3  **13**

5  **15**

1  **11**

 What order did the machine follow?

What order would you give the FM?

27

Nutty Questions

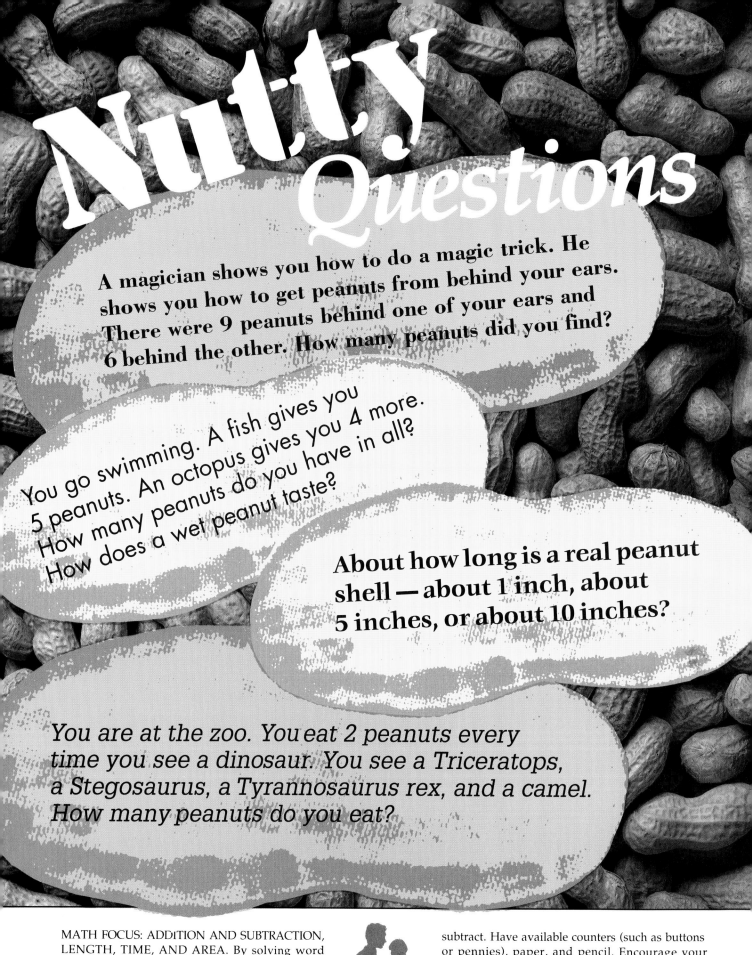

A magician shows you how to do a magic trick. He shows you how to get peanuts from behind your ears. There were 9 peanuts behind one of your ears and 6 behind the other. How many peanuts did you find?

You go swimming. A fish gives you 5 peanuts. An octopus gives you 4 more. How many peanuts do you have in all? How does a wet peanut taste?

About how long is a real peanut shell — about 1 inch, about 5 inches, or about 10 inches?

You are at the zoo. You eat 2 peanuts every time you see a dinosaur. You see a Triceratops, a Stegosaurus, a Tyrannosaurus rex, and a camel. How many peanuts do you eat?

MATH FOCUS: ADDITION AND SUBTRACTION, LENGTH, TIME, AND AREA. By solving word problems, children learn to reason mathematically while applying several mathematical concepts and skills. They also decide when to add and when to subtract. Have available counters (such as buttons or pennies), paper, and pencil. Encourage your child to tell you how he or she solved the problems.

28

A monkey can eat 10 peanuts in one minute. How many peanuts can he eat in two minutes?

You find 10 peanuts in your shoe. Your dog eats 3 of them. How many peanuts are left in your shoe? Who will eat them?

An elephant comes to your house for lunch. You give him 20 peanuts on a plate. The elephant eats 18 of them. How many are left for you? What is a good name for the elephant?

About how many peanuts would you need to cover one page of this book — about 10, about 20, or about 100?

There were 15 peanuts lying in the road. After an elephant walked across the road, there were only 5 peanuts left. How many peanuts turned into peanut butter?

MORE FUN. Taking turns with your child, make up and answer your own nutty questions. Have family members try to solve them.

HOLD THE ANCHOVIES

Professor Guesser glanced at the clock. It was 7:55. She searched through the morning newspaper and found the ad she had placed the day before:

Professor Guesser
No problem too big or too small
for Professor Guesser to solve.
Call 555-MEOW after 8 o'clock.

At 8:00 sharp the phone rang. It was Pepper Pepperoni. He was frantic. "Professor Guesser, come right away!" he begged. "What's the problem?" asked the professor.

MATH FOCUS: GEOMETRY. By seeing pictures of plane shapes (circle, square, triangle, rectangle) and their corresponding solid shapes (sphere, cube, octahedron, rectangular prism), children sharpen their awareness of the geometry in everyday objects. Help your child see the relationship between each solid shape and its corresponding plane shape—for example, cube and square.

"Problem? I've got problems in every shape and size—all covered with anchovies!" Before Pepper could finish, Professor Guesser grabbed her detective kit and ran out the door. She loved anchovies!

She arrived at Pepper's pizza truck while Pepper was still talking.

"Where are the anchovies?" asked Professor Guesser.

"How did you get here so fast?" asked Pepper.

"Never mind that. What about those anchovies?" the professor asked again.

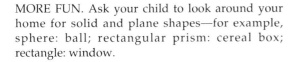

MORE FUN. Ask your child to look around your home for solid and plane shapes—for example, sphere: ball; rectangular prism: cereal box; rectangle: window.

"The anchovies are on the floor!" said Pepper. "Let me start at the beginning. I take orders for pizza circles. I take orders for pizza triangles, pizza rectangles, and pizza squares, too. I spread one cup of sauce on the dough. I sprinkle on two cups of cheese, and I put 10 tiny anchovies on top. Then I cook them in my brand-new pizza oven."

"So what's the problem?" asked Professor Guesser.

"Something mysterious has happened. When I take the pizzas out of the oven, they're all puffed up. I get pizza spheres, pizza octahedrons, and pizza rectangular prisms. I even get pizza cubes!" wailed Pepper.

"This is serious!" said Professor Guesser.

"It sure is," said Pepper. "But that's not the only problem."

"There's more?" asked Professor Guesser.

"When the pizza shapes puff up, I have no idea which pizza belongs to which order because the shapes are all different. And, worst of all, the anchovies slide off the pizza," said Pepper. "How can I sell pizzas without anchovies?"

"How puzzling," said Professor Guesser. "You really do have problems. Let me take a look."

Professor Guesser carefully looked at the pizza oven in the truck. "It looks like a normal pizza oven to me. Maybe if we change the recipe that might solve the problem," she suggested.

sphere

rectangular prism

octahedron

cube

What do an octahedron and an octopus have in common?
An octahedron has 8 sides and an octopus has 8 arms.

"Good idea," said Pepper. "Let me get my measuring cups. You can watch me to see if anything strange happens."

"OK," said Professor Guesser.

So Pepper made a pizza in the shape of a circle. Then he put one cup of sauce on it. He sprinkled two cups of cheese on top of the sauce. He finished by arranging 10 tiny anchovies very neatly on top.

circle

rectangle

Pepper followed the same steps with triangular pizza dough, rectangular pizza dough, and square pizza dough. Then he put them all into the oven, set the speed, and waited.

"Looks fine so far," said Professor Guesser.

I'm really hungry! I could eat a pizza twice that size. I wonder how much sauce and cheese would be needed if the recipe were doubled. How many anchovies would be on it?

triangle

square

35

In just a few minutes, the pizzas were done. Pepper carefully opened the oven door and peeked inside. "Oh, no! They're still puffed up!" he cried.

"Well, it can't be the recipe," said Professor Guesser. "It must be something else. What else did you do differently?"

"I cooked them on super-duper hyperspeed," said Pepper. "I wanted them to cook really fast so the people who ordered them wouldn't have to wait very long."

"Well, that's thoughtful," said Professor Guesser.

What will this be when it's all puffed up?

"But it only made problems for me,"said Pepper. "Just look at all these ruined pizzas!" he cried. "No one will want them. They're not flat, and there are no anchovies on any of them. "

"Look at the manual for your new oven," said the professor.

"Wow! Listen to this!" said Pepper, and he read out loud from the manual.

"CAUTION! PUSHING THE SUPER-DUPER HYPERSPEED BUTTON COULD RESULT IN PUFFED-UP BAKED GOODS."

"Now we know why the pizzas puffed up—because they cooked too quickly," said Professor Guesser. "And I'm pretty sure that people will want them. After all, they are the only ones of their kind in the city!"

*Do you know which shape each
flat pizza puffed into?*

"That's true," said Pepper. "But I don't know which pizza to give to which customer."

"Let's look closely at the new solid pizzas," said Professor Guesser. "Doesn't this pizza sphere look like a puffed-up circle? And this one is an octahedron shape. It's made of triangles."

"That's true," said Pepper.

"If you look at this pizza," said Professor Guesser, "you'll see that it's a rectangular prism. All of its sides are shaped like rectangles. And this cube pizza has sides shaped like squares. Now you know exactly which pizza to give to which customer."

"Fabulous!" exclaimed Pepper. "Step right up!" he called to the customers who had been waiting for their pizzas. "Try the new Shapey's solid pizzas. Forget flat circles. Eat a pizza sphere. Try a new angle. Eat an octahedron pizza. Try a rectangular prism pizza, too. And don't be square—eat a pizza cube!"

"Delicious!" said a customer. "And so much better without those salty little fish. I'm glad you decided to hold the anchovies. I'll be back for more solid pizza tomorrow."

"Thank you, professor," said Pepper. "You've solved my problem. You really are a wonderful problem solver."

"You're welcome," said Professor Guesser, "but now you have another problem. You have all these anchovies to get rid of."

Pepper smiled. "Oh, I can solve that problem! You can have them if they're not too heavy for you to carry."

"No matter how heavy they are," said Professor Guesser, "I can always hold the anchovies!"

Cut It Out!

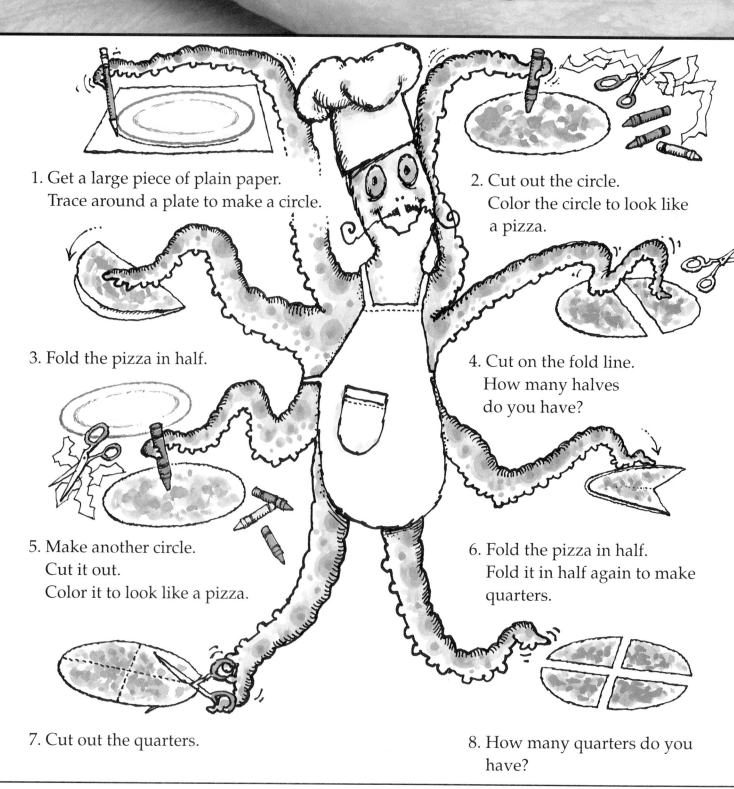

1. Get a large piece of plain paper. Trace around a plate to make a circle.

2. Cut out the circle. Color the circle to look like a pizza.

3. Fold the pizza in half.

4. Cut on the fold line. How many halves do you have?

5. Make another circle. Cut it out. Color it to look like a pizza.

6. Fold the pizza in half. Fold it in half again to make quarters.

7. Cut out the quarters.

8. How many quarters do you have?

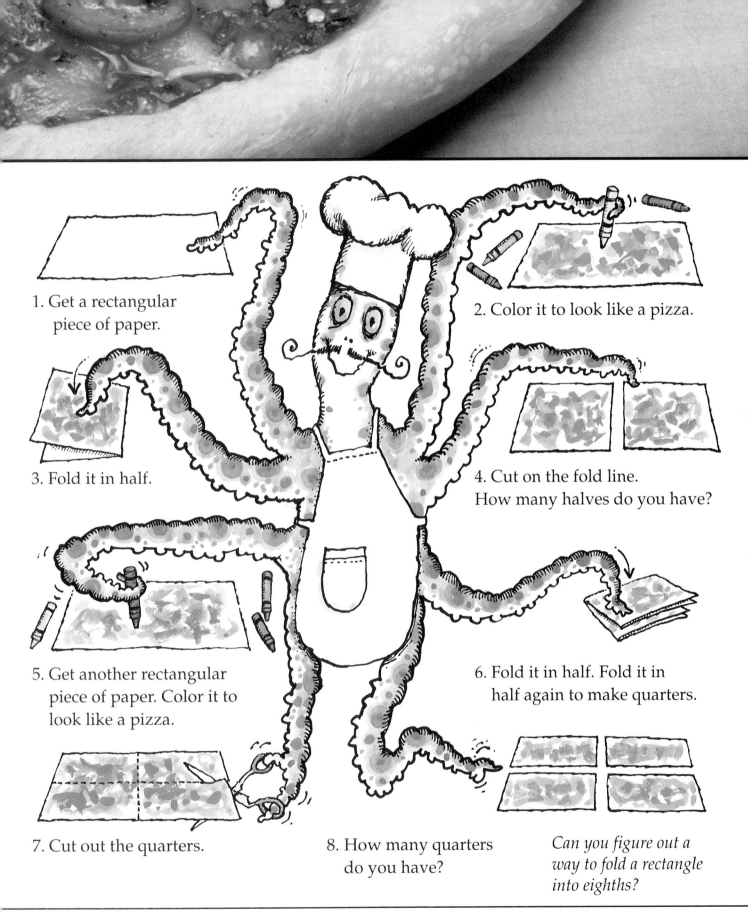

1. Get a rectangular piece of paper.

2. Color it to look like a pizza.

3. Fold it in half.

4. Cut on the fold line. How many halves do you have?

5. Get another rectangular piece of paper. Color it to look like a pizza.

6. Fold it in half. Fold it in half again to make quarters.

7. Cut out the quarters.

8. How many quarters do you have?

Can you figure out a way to fold a rectangle into eighths?

MORE FUN. Help your child cut an apple into halves and another apple into quarters. Discuss the concept of equal parts and the fact that "the bigger half" is really impossible.

How do butterflies count french fries?

One day four hungry butterflies,
Found a hefty box of fries.

"I think that we should each have two!"

"I think that six apiece will do."

"I want to eat them all!" one said.

But then the blue one used her head.

"Let's put the french fries in a line.
Then we can tally them just fine.
We can count them up to see,
How to divide them evenly."

She tried and tried and soon was able,
To put ONE french fry on the table.

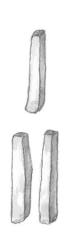

The other butterflies helped, too.
Now on the table there were TWO!

MATH FOCUS: TALLYING. By seeing pictures of tallied groups of five or more, children learn how tallying can be of help when they are counting quantities of objects.

Point out that the fifth french fry in each group of five is the diagonal one. Help your child work out how many french fries each butterfly gets.

They put more french fries in a bunch,
THREE, FOUR, FIVE to eat for lunch.

Five plus one more made it SIX.
They lined them up like counting sticks.

SEVEN, EIGHT and NINE and TEN.
Two groups of five were tallied then.

Two more groups of five made TWENTY.
They could see that there were plenty.

So then they all sat down to eat
A fairly split-up french-fry treat.
Each butterfly got the same amount.
How many, you say? Take a count.

MORE FUN. Have your child take a handful of straws, guess how many there are, make tallying groups, and then count by fives. Any single straws left over should be added to the tallied amount to get a total.

The Three Mathcateers to the RESCUE

It was almost 6 o'clock in the evening. Alexander hopped home unaware of the terrible trouble that lay ahead. It had already been a difficult and disappointing day. Around 9 o'clock that morning he had been shooed from a lettuce patch. At noon he was chased by a fox. He spent three hours in the afternoon crouched under a wooden crate waiting for Mrs. Bixby's old black cat to finish her nap. When she finally woke up, Alexander was free, but very hungry. He hadn't eaten so much as a nibble and was beginning to feel a little faint.

MATH FOCUS: LOGICAL THINKING, ADDITION AND SUBTRACTION, AND SPATIAL RELATIONSHIPS. By solving riddles, children learn to analyze information and to apply

44

reasoning skills. On pages 48–49, have your child use a finger to trace the path of the rabbit through the garden.

At a turn in the road, the smell of a vegetable garden revived him. Alexander looked at the brick wall that separated him from supper and moaned, "I'm famished. I wish I had wings. My legs won't take me over that wall. It must be 10 feet high." Then he saw something, something incredible—a hole big enough for a rabbit to squeeze through.

Alexander popped through to the other side, sat up, and rubbed his eyes. He couldn't believe what he saw. Bathed in the beautiful pink and orange twilight were rows and rows of green beans, lima beans, eggplants, pumpkins, peppers, tomatoes, corn, squash, watermelon, and sweet potatoes. Best of all, the farmer was nowhere in sight.

Alexander ate to his heart's content. He ate 3 green beans. He gobbled 1 tasty red tomato. He nibbled 2 ears of corn and 4 delicious sweet potatoes.

How many vegetables did that rabbit eat?

Alexander couldn't eat another bite. It was 8 o'clock and getting dark. He really had to be getting home. Alexander put some peppers, beans, and tomatoes in a sack to take with him. He hopped back to the wall and was just about to wriggle through the hole when something tapped him on the shoulder. "Going somewhere?" asked a deep voice.

Alexander shrieked, dropped his sack of goodies, and ran as fast as he could through the sweet potatoes, over the cucumbers, under the beans, across the peppers, and between the pumpkins. The farmer's scarecrow followed closely behind.

Luckily, three brave fireflies—Flash, Wink, and Blink—heard the rabbit's cry.

"It's time for a firefly surprise!" said Wink.

"Light makes right!" called Blink.

"Fireflies to the rescue!" shouted Flash.

Out of the sky they flew like bolts of lightning. They zipped around the scarecrow in circles of flashing light.

Sweet Potatoes

Alexander then darted through some squash and ran into the farmer's shed. The scarecrow and the fireflies chased after him.

"I've got you now!" said the scarecrow as he snared the rabbit in his net.

"Not if we can help it!" said Flash.

"Let him go," said Blink. "We mean business!"

"I will let him go on one condition," said the scarecrow. "If you're so concerned about saving your little friend, you must each solve a riddle, and the rabbit may not help. If you fail, I will give him to the farmer, and you know what that means."

"Three riddles for the three best riddle-solving fireflies in the galaxy," said Flash. "Let's get started!"

"Very well. Let's see how bright you really are," said the scarecrow. He got four packets of seeds and lined them up on the table. "Here's the first riddle," he said.

**"Which packet of seeds am I thinking of?
It has more than 3 letters but fewer than 5.
It starts with the letter C."**

Can you guess which packet of seeds the scarecrow is thinking of?

51

"The first clue means there must be 4 letters in the word," reasoned Flash. "So it must be corn or peas. But which one is it? Let me think."

Alexander cried, "If you have a single *kernel* of decency, you'll remind the firefly of the second part of the clue. I don't want to be popped into a pot of stew!"

Wink understood Alexander's hint and flew in the air behind the scarecrow's back. Wink flashed the letter C to begin the word.

"I know! I know! CORN! Corn has more than 3 letters but fewer than 5, and it begins with C," said Flash.

"You're right. But let's see if you can shine with my next riddle," said the scarecrow. He got a handful of beans and spread them across the table. Then he covered some with a flowerpot. "Listen carefully," he said.

"There are 20 beans in all. How many of the beans are under the pot?"

Wink studied the problem carefully. "I don't know how many beans are under the pot," she said. "I can see only the ones that are around the pot."

How many beans do you think are under the pot?

"If you don't answer correctly, you can count on one thing—the scarecrow will subtract me from this planet," said Alexander.

Blink and Flash counted the number of beans in each group next to the flowerpot. Then they wrote two number sentences in the dirt behind the scarecrow and lit them up so Wink could see them. She saw the answer at once.

"I knew it all along. There are 20 beans in all. There are 10 beans around the pot. So there must be 10 beans under the pot," said Wink.

3 + 7 = 10
20 - 10 = 10

"Remarkable," said the scarecrow to Blink. "But the next time, your problem will be very puzzling indeed."

The scarecrow got a pumpkin from the garden and a knife from the shed. He cut the pumpkin into pieces to look like a jigsaw puzzle. He laid the pieces in the tray, with one piece missing. Then the scarecrow showed Blink three other puzzle pieces. "You'll never get this one!" he cackled.

"Which of these pieces fits exactly into the empty space?"

Which puzzle piece do you think Blink will choose?

"Hurry, please! I'm just the right shape to fit into the farmer's roasting pan," moaned Alexander.

Blink whispered to the other fireflies, "No need to help me on this one, my friends. Stay where you are and watch the scarecrow squirm."

Blink stood up straight and said in his loudest voice, "I know the answer just by looking at the shape of the empty space." He picked up the piece marked A and put it into the pumpkin puzzle. It fit perfectly.

The scarecrow lifted the net, and Alexander scurried out of the shed. The scarecrow called out, "Don't ever let me catch you in my garden again!"

"You won't!" shouted Alexander as he and the fireflies raced through the hole in the wall.

Back at his burrow, Alexander and his new friends sipped tea and ate the food from the sack he remembered to rescue on his way out of the garden.

Riddles to Go

The scarecrow sees three flowers.
Which flower does he like best?
It has 5 petals.
It has 3 leaves.
It has a yellow center.

On a piece of paper, try drawing the vegetables. Use yellow, red, and green crayons.

The scarecrow put a vegetable under each shell.
A corn kernel is under the shell on the left.
A radish is under the shell to the left of the shell that a green pea is under.
Which vegetable is under the middle shell?

MATH FOCUS: LOGICAL THINKING, ADDITION AND SUBTRACTION. Have available paper, pencils, crayons, and counters.

MORE FUN. Have your child create his or her own riddles and challenge family members to solve them.

What seed package does
the scarecrow want?
It has 4 flowers on it.
It does not have a blue flower.

You can use buttons
or pennies to work
this one out.

Try using buttons
for this one, too.

The scarecrow had 7 beans.
Alexander had 4 beans.
The scarecrow gave 2 of his
beans to Alexander.
Who had more beans then?

The scarecrow wants the same
number of tomatoes in each group.
How many tomatoes must he
move from the group on the left to
the group on the right?

Secret Numbers

My secret number is greater than

It is less than

It is not

What is my secret number?

My secret number is greater than

It is less than

It has a   in it.

What is my secret number?

My secret number has two digits.

It is less than a dozen.

It is not

What is my secret number?

MATH FOCUS: LOGICAL THINKING. Children learn to analyze information and use the process of elimination to solve these problems. Have available paper and pencil.

MORE FUN. Have your child create his or her own "secret number" problems and challenge family members to solve them.

My secret number is greater than the number of

legs on an octopus.

It is less than the number of toes on a person's feet.

What is my secret number?

My secret number is greater than

It is less than

Both digits in my number are the same.

What is my secret number?

My secret number is less than the number of eggs

in half a dozen.

It is more than your number of ears.

It does not begin with F.

What is my secret number?

CALCULATOR FUN

OH! IT'S ZERO!

Pick a number from 1 to 10.
Enter your number on the calculator.
Add 3.
Subtract 2.
Add 4.
Subtract 5.
Subtract the number you started with and then press =.

Try this trick a few times. Use a different number each time. I bet your answer will always be zero!

PICK A NUMBER!

Pick a number from 11 to 20.
Enter your number on the calculator.
Add 10.
Add 5.
Subtract 8.
Subtract 7 and then press =.

See if the last number on the calculator screen is the same as the number you started with.

MATH FOCUS: ADDITION AND SUBTRACTION. By performing number tricks on a calculator, children practice addition and subtraction. Have available a basic calculator with large keys.

Ask your child to look carefully at the steps and discuss why he or she thinks you get the same answer every time.

FIVE ALIVE!

Pick a number from 6 to 16.
Enter it on the calculator.
Add 1.
Subtract 2.
Add 3.
Subtract 4.
Add 5.
Subtract 6.
Add 7.
Subtract 8.
Add 9.
Subtract the number you started with and then press =.

Now try this one a few times and see what happens.

IT'S MAGIC!

Pick a number from 7 to 17.
Enter it on the calculator.
Add 5.
Add 5.
Add 5.
Add 5.
Subtract 10.
Subtract 10 and then press =.

Try this with a different number. Do you always get the number you started with?

MORE FUN. Ask your child to try these tricks with family members. Your child may also create his or her own calculator tricks.

TIME-LIFE for CHILDREN™

Publisher: Robert H. Smith
Associate Publisher and Managing Editor: Neil Kagan
Assistant Managing Editor: Patricia Daniels
Editorial Directors: Jean Burke Crawford, Allan Fallow,
　Karin Kinney, Sara Mark, Elizabeth Ward
Director of Marketing: Margaret Mooney
Product Managers: Cassandra Ford,
　Shelley L. Schimkus
Director of Finance: Lisa Peterson
Financial Analyst: Patricia Vanderslice
Administrative Assistant: Barbara A. Jones
Production Manager: Prudence G. Harris
Production: Celia Beattie
Supervisor of Quality Control: James King

Produced by Kirchoff/Wohlberg, Inc.
866 United Nations Plaza,
New York, New York 10017

Series Director: Mary Jane Martin
Creative Director: Morris A. Kirchoff
Mathematics Director: Jo Dennis
Designer: Jessica A. Kirchoff
Assistant Designers: Brian Collins, Mariah Corrigan,
　Ann Eitzen, Judith Schwartz
Contributing Writers: Alice Benjamin Boynton,
　Anne M. Miranda
Managing Editor: Nancy Pernick
Editors: Susan Darwin, Beth Grout, David McCoy

Cover Illustration: Roberta Holmes

Illustration Credits: Bob Barner, pp. 6–7; Liz Callen,
pp. 8–15, p. 60; Brian Cody, pp. 16–17; Dara Goldman,
pp. 44–60; Rosekrans Hoffman, pp. 42–43, p. 61;
Susan Jaekel, pp. 18–19, p. 61; Tom Leonard, pp. 20–27,
pp. 62–63; Don Madden, pp. 30–41, p. 61, end papers;
Carol Nicklaus, end papers; Sharron O'Neil, pp. 60–61

Photography Credits: R. Emery/FPG International,
pp. 40–41; Justin Kirchoff, p. 16, pp. 28–29

First printing. Printed in U.S.A.
Published simultaneously in Canada.

Time Life Inc. is a wholly owned subsidiary of THE TIME INC.
BOOK COMPANY

TIME-LIFE is a trademark of Time Warner Inc. U.S.A.

For subscription information, call 1-800-621-7026.

CONSULTANTS

Mary Jane Martin spent 17 years working in elementary
school classrooms as a teacher and reading consultant; for
seven of those years she was a first-grade teacher. The
second half of her career has been devoted to publishing.
During this time she has helped create and produce a wide
variety of innovative elementary programs, including two
mathematics textbook series.

Jo Dennis has worked as a teacher and math consultant in
England, Australia, and the United States for more than 20
years. Most recently, she has helped develop and write
several mathematics textbooks for kindergarten, first grade,
and second grade.

Catherine Motz Peterson is a curriculum specialist
who spent five years developing an early elementary
mathematics program for the nationally acclaimed Fairfax
County Public Schools in Virginia. She is also mathematics
consultant to the University Of Maryland, Catholic
University, and the Fredrick County Public Schools in
Maryland. Ms. Peterson is the director of the Capitol
Hill Day School in Washington, D.C.

Library of Congress Cataloging-in-Publication Data

How do octopi eat pizza pie? : pizza math.
　　　p.　cm. —— (I love math)
　　　Summary: A collection of stories, poems, games,
and activities, all focusing on food, introduce such basic
mathematical skills as number awareness, addition,
subtraction, and estimation.
　　　ISBN 0-8094-9950-9
　　　1. Mathematics—Juvenile literature. 2. Food—
Juvenile literature. [1. Mathematics. 2. Mathematical
recreations. 3. Food—Miscellanea.] I. Time-Life for Children
(Firm) II. Series.
QA40.5.H66　　1992
510—dc20　　　　　　　　　　92-16839
　　　　　　　　　　　　　　　CIP
　　　　　　　　　　　　　　　AC

TIC-TAC-PIZZA

THE NUMBER OF PLAYERS:

The Object of the Game: To get three pieces in a straight line, as in tic-tac-toe. To cover larger numbers for a higher score.

The Playing Pieces: Five for each player—for example, macaroni for one player, jelly beans for the other.
Note: There are four game boards.

The Play: The first player chooses a game board and puts a playing piece on any space. Players take turns placing one piece at a time on the chosen game board. Play stops when a player gets three pieces in a line—vertically, horizontally, or diagonally—or when all the spaces are covered.

The Winner: Each player removes his or her pieces and adds the uncovered numbers, scoring two extra points if he or she had three pieces in a line.

The player with the higher score wins.

Math Concepts: Addition with sums from 3 to 24. Adding 3 or more numbers.